LOST CITIES

Contents

Jan Burchett
and Sara Vogler

Story illustrated by
Tom Percival

Heinemann

Before Reading

Find out about

- What happened to the city of Pompeii in AD 79

Tricky words

- Pompeii (say *Pom-pay-ee*)
- Mount Vesuvius
- erupt
- explosion
- jewellery
- buried
- choked
- archaeologists

Introduce these tricky words and help the reader when they come across them later!

Text starter

Two thousand years ago, there was a Roman city called Pompeii. It was close to a volcano called Mount Vesuvius. The people were not afraid of living so close to an active volcano. No one thought it would ever erupt.

The Lost City of Pompeii

The city of Pompeii was close to a volcano called Mount Vesuvius. Sometimes the people heard strange sounds and saw smoke coming from the volcano. Sometimes the ground shook. But no one thought that the volcano would erupt. Everyone just went on with their lives.

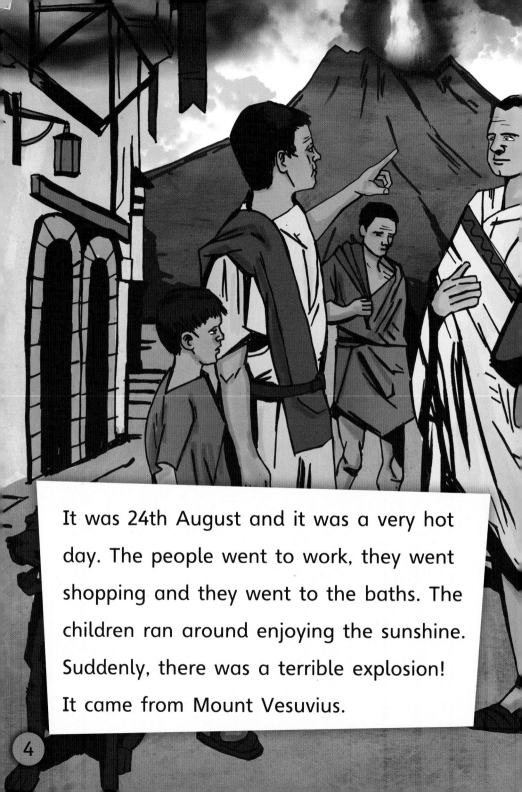

It was 24th August and it was a very hot day. The people went to work, they went shopping and they went to the baths. The children ran around enjoying the sunshine. Suddenly, there was a terrible explosion! It came from Mount Vesuvius.

The people looked at the volcano and saw a huge cloud of black ash shooting out of the top of it. Then the ash spread out like a huge umbrella. There were flashes like lightning and the people could hear a loud rumbling sound. It was the boiling hot ash pouring out of Vesuvius.

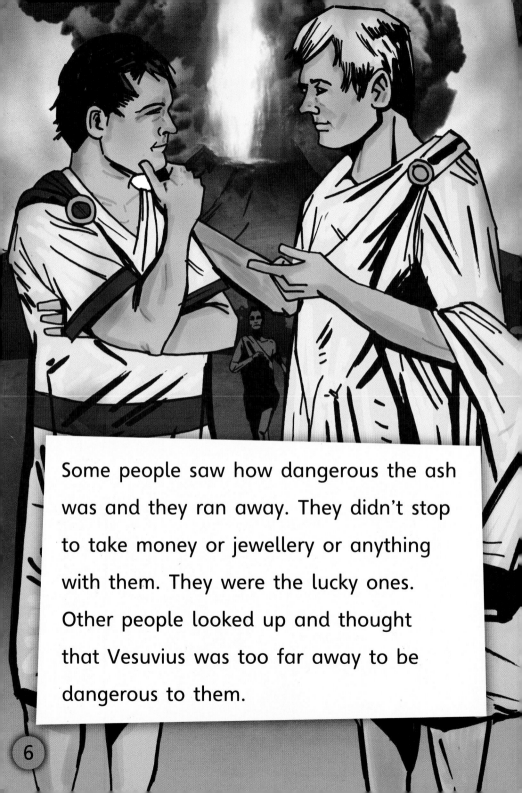

Some people saw how dangerous the ash was and they ran away. They didn't stop to take money or jewellery or anything with them. They were the lucky ones. Other people looked up and thought that Vesuvius was too far away to be dangerous to them.

Suddenly, rocks and stones came shooting out from Vesuvius and fell down on to Pompeii. They crushed some houses and the people were trapped inside. They tried to escape but it was too late and they were buried alive.

The hot ash and stones spread over the whole city. There was nowhere that people could hide to get away from the boiling ash that fell like rain. Men, women, children, babies and animals breathed the ash into their lungs and they choked and died.

How do we know so much about what happened? A famous Roman writer called Pliny was living near Pompeii. When the eruption happened he wanted to help people but there was nothing he could do. Later, he wrote down all the terrible things he had seen.

Pliny wrote that he saw a huge black cloud with flashes of fire in it. He saw the sea being sucked away and fish left flapping on the sand. He saw the hot ash and stones falling on the city. He wrote that the day was as dark as night. About 20,000 people died on that terrible day.

By 25th August the city of Pompeii had disappeared. It was buried under the stones and ash for over 1,500 years. Then archaeologists started to dig. They had to dig through many layers of stones and ash to find the streets and houses that had been buried when Vesuvius erupted.

What do you think the archaeologists found?

The archaeologists found some strange holes in the ash that looked like the shapes of bodies. Then they knew what they had found. The hot ash had cooled around the bodies of the people and animals of Pompeii. When their bodies rotted away, their shapes were left in the ash.

The archaeologists poured some plaster into the holes. When the plaster was hard, it formed the shapes of the people who had died. Some people had been sitting at tables and some had money and jewellery in their hands.

They all looked as if they had died in terrible pain.

Mount Vesuvius is an active volcano. It could erupt again at any time! But this time people will be ready. They have machines to tell them when an eruption is coming. They will try to escape but will they be quick enough this time?

Quiz

Text Detective

- What happened to the city of Pompeii?
- Why did the archaeologists pour plaster into the holes?

Word Detective

- **Phonic Focus:** Vowel phonemes in polysyllabic words

  Page 3: How many syllables are there in 'volcano'?
  What vowel phoneme can you hear in each syllable?

- Page 5: Find three adjectives describing the eruption
  (e.g. huge, loud, rumbling).

- Page 14: Which word tells us that Vesuvius could
  erupt again? (active)

Super Speller

Read these words:

everyone   nowhere   escape

Now try to spell them!

HA! HA! HA!

Q What did one volcano say to the other volcano?

A I lava you!

Before Reading

In this story

 Carla

 Rob

 Dad

 Introduce these tricky words and help the reader when they come across them later!

Tricky words

- search
- scared
- museum
- huge
- earthquake
- beware
- statues
- gasped

Story starter

Carla's and Rob's dad is an archaeologist. He finds out about people who lived long ago. One summer, Carla and Rob went with their dad to search for the ancient underwater city of Atlantis. They hired a boat and diving gear and set off to where the lost city was supposed to be.

In Search of Atlantis

Carla and Rob helped Dad get ready to dive. He was going to search for the lost city of Atlantis.

"Can we dive with you?" asked Rob.

"OK," said Dad. "But you must stay close to me."

They searched and searched but did not find Atlantis.

When they got back to the boat Rob said to Carla, "Wasn't it spooky down there? I thought someone was following us."

"You're just chicken," said Carla. "I wasn't scared at all."

Carla and Rob wanted to find out about Atlantis.

"Go to the museum in the town," said Dad, "and ask someone there."

Carla and Rob went to the museum.

"Can you tell us the legend of the lost city of Atlantis?" said Carla.

The man said that Atlantis was once on land but the people of the city were bad. Their god made a huge earthquake and the city sank under the sea.

"Did all the people drown?" asked Carla.
"No," said the man. "The legend says
they lived on in their underwater city
but sometimes they come up to the
town. They are strange people with
gills in their necks, just like fish. But
beware, bad things have happened to
people who search for Atlantis!"

"That was a spooky story," said Rob.

"Maybe it's not safe to dive."

"I'm not scared," said Carla. "It's just

a story!"

Suddenly Rob grabbed her arm. "Look at

that strange woman. Maybe she's from

the lost city and she's got that scarf to

hide the gills on her neck!"

"Rubbish!" said Carla.

They went back to find Dad. He was getting ready to dive again.

"I'll come with you," said Carla. "But Rob thinks the stories about Atlantis are true and he's scared."

"I'm not scared. I'm coming too!" shouted Rob.

They dived down again.

Rob swam off on his own. He would
show Carla he wasn't scared.

But suddenly there was an ugly face
looking at him from a rock! Rob's heart
thumped. Was it one of the strange
people of Atlantis?

Rob looked again. No, it was just an eel. The eel gave him an idea. He decided to play a trick on Carla. He waved Carla over to where the eel was. Suddenly the eel shot out at her. Carla swam off in fright.

"Great trick!" thought Rob as he swam after her.

He came to a strange stone arch.

"What can this be?" he thought as he swam through it. Then he stopped dead.

What do you think Rob has found?

There in front of him were stone walls
and strange statues.

"Wow!" thought Rob. "This must be the
lost city of Atlantis!"

Then he felt a tap on his back. He spun
round. It was Carla. She was looking
amazed too.

Suddenly they saw a dark shape above them. They looked up to see something falling through the water. It was a huge, stone head.

Rob and Carla tried to swim away but the stone face bashed Carla on the arm.

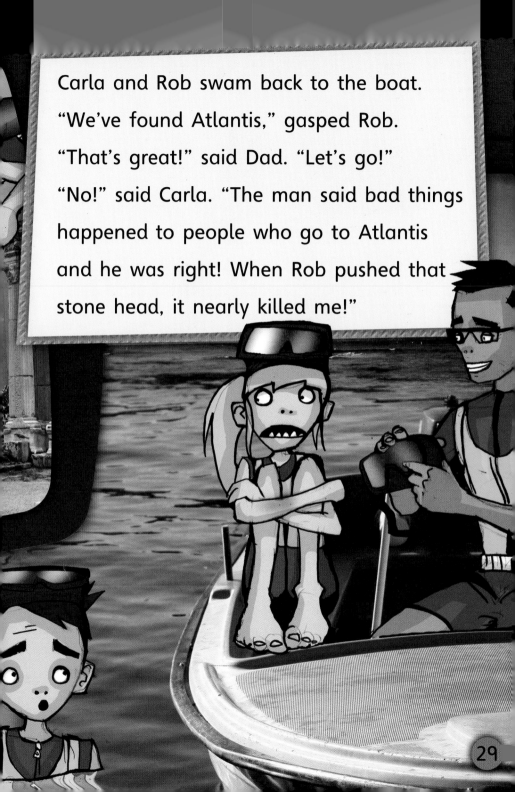

Carla and Rob swam back to the boat.

"We've found Atlantis," gasped Rob.

"That's great!" said Dad. "Let's go!"

"No!" said Carla. "The man said bad things happened to people who go to Atlantis and he was right! When Rob pushed that stone head, it nearly killed me!"

"I didn't push it," said Rob. "I thought **you** were playing a trick on me after I scared you with the eel!"

"Maybe the eel moved the head?" said Carla.

"Or there was someone down there," said Rob quietly, "someone who did not want us in their city!"

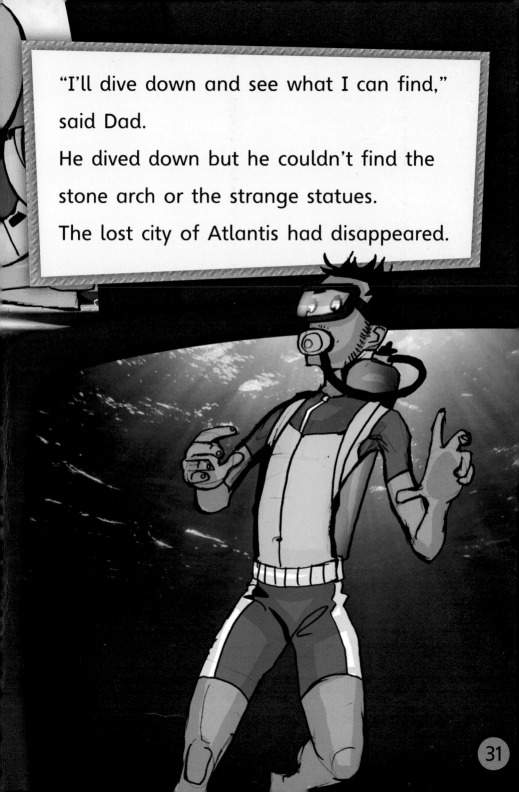

"I'll dive down and see what I can find," said Dad.

He dived down but he couldn't find the stone arch or the strange statues.

The lost city of Atlantis had disappeared.

Quiz

Text Detective

- Why did Rob play a trick on Carla?
- Do you believe the legend of Atlantis?

Word Detective

- **Phonic Focus:** Vowel phonemes in polysyllabic words

  Page 17: Sound out the four phonemes in 'close'. Which letters make the long vowel phoneme?
- Page 19: What words does Dad say?
- Page 19: Find a word made from two small words.

Super Speller

Read these words:

ready coming above

Now try to spell them!

HA! HA! HA!

Q What do you get when you cross a cow with an earthquake?

A A milkshake!